Super Instruments

by Abbie Rushton

What is an Orchestra?

This is a school orchestra. The children play lots of super fun instruments.

a school orchestra

Let's look at the different parts of an orchestra.

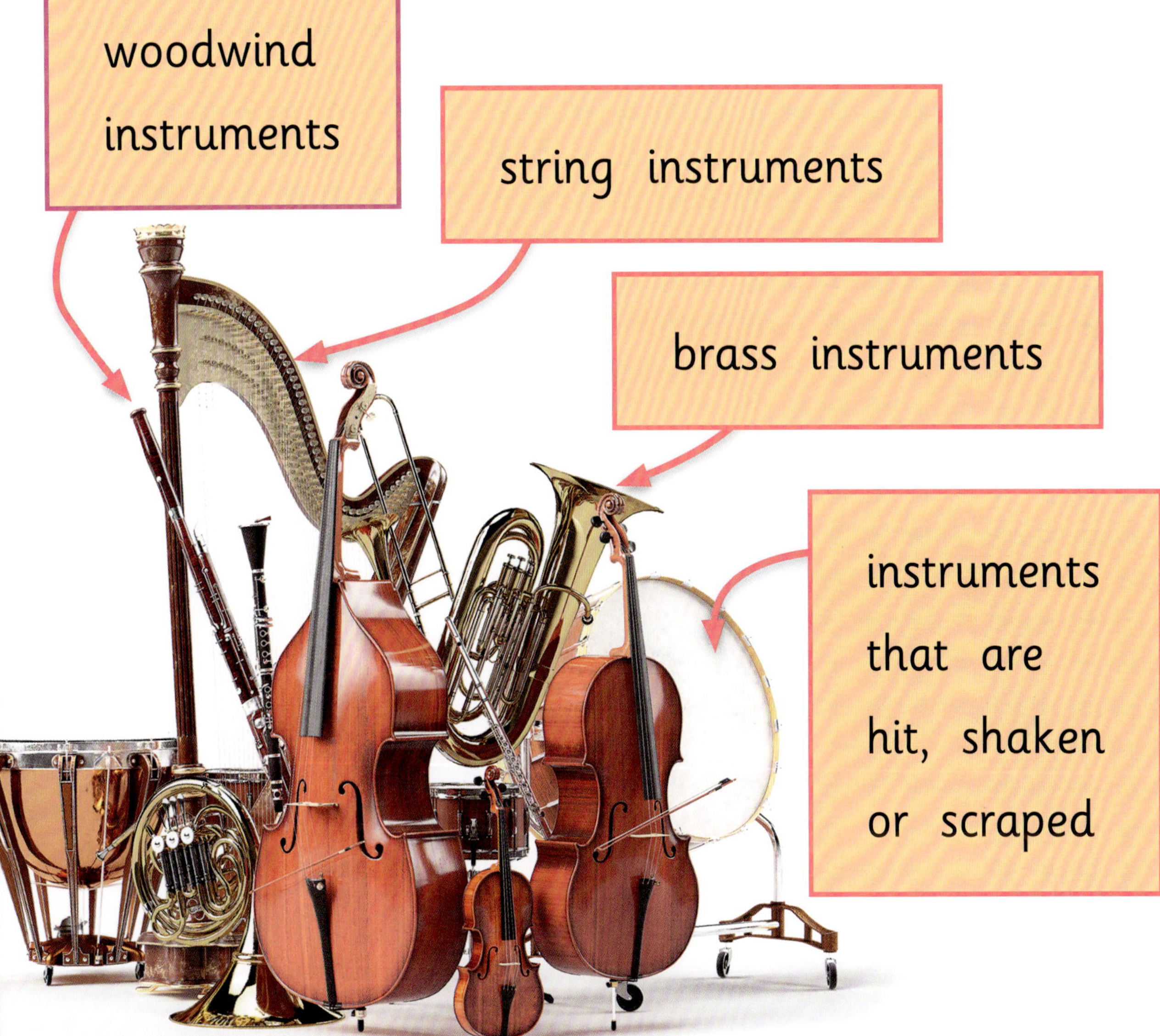

String Instruments

String instruments make music when their strings **vibrate**.

A violin rests under your chin. You rub a bow on the strings.

Violins are made from about 70 bits of wood. Different woods are used in different parts.

tuning peg

string

chin rest

The harp is one of the oldest instruments. Most harps have 47 strings. Harps also have pedals which alter the sound.

A harpist leans the grand instrument against their body. They pluck or **strum** the strings. The music is pleasant and relaxing.

Woodwind Instruments

You blow into woodwind instruments.

Hold the flute to the side of your head.
Take a deep breath. Blow and push the keys.

Flutes are also very old instruments.

Super Fact!

The flute may be the oldest instrument ever found!

This flute is made from bone.

Clarinets are reed instruments. A reed is a thin bit of wood or metal. When air passes over the reed, it vibrates. This makes a sound.

People get oboes and clarinets mixed up. Here are some ways they are different.

Oboe	Clarinet
two reeds	one reed
rounded bell	wider bell

Brass Instruments

Brass instrument players vibrate their lips.

To play the trumpet, make a buzzing sound. Push the buttons on top.

Trombones are also brass instruments. Trombones are longer and larger than trumpets. You slide a tube to make different sounds.

Tubas can be very big. You usually have to sit down to play a tuba. It can rest on your lap or a stool.

Super Fact!

Brass instruments were not always made of the metal brass. In the past, wood, bone or animal horns were used.

a trumpet made of bone

Hit, Shaken or Scraped Instruments

These are noisy instruments! People use their hands or sticks to play them.

Marimba

A marimba is made of wooden bars. The bars have pipes under them. It is played with a mallet.

Drum

The bass drum is the biggest drum. It can be hit by pushing a pedal.

The bass drum makes a low sound.

Triangle

The triangle hangs from a loop. It is hit with a stick. The triangle makes a tinging sound.

Time for a Show!

This school orchestra puts on a show. They have been practising for weeks. The **chorus** is a bit tricky.

school orchestra

Lots of people's family and friends have come. The brochure includes the name of everyone in the orchestra.

The hall is full.

The orchestra puts on their show.

What a fantastic job! The orchestra take a bow.

Everyone enjoyed it.

You could join an orchestra too.

You can learn a new skill. You might even make some new friends.

Which instrument would you play?

Glossary

chorus: a part of a song that is repeated

strum: to run your fingers along the strings

vibrate: to shake from side to side quickly

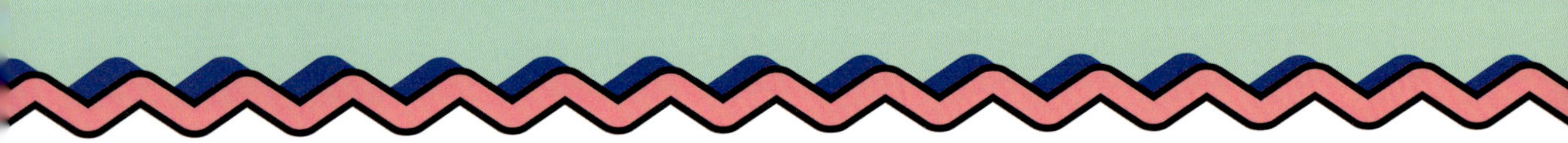

Index